010885

THE SEASONS SEWN

A YEAR IN PATCHWORK

Written by

Ann Whitford Paul

Illustrated by

Michael McCurdy

BROWNDEER PRESS

HARCOURT BRACE & COMPANY

San Diego   New York   London

For Ron,
with love in every season
—A. W. P.

Special thanks go to Dorothy Helfeld and all the other wonderful librarians who have listened
to my questions, sent me to the right book, dug deep in their research files, and found an
answer even when I was sure there was none. Thanks, too, to Sandi Fox, formerly the collection
curator of quilts, costumes, and textiles at the Los Angeles County Museum of Art in
Los Angeles, California, who took the time and trouble to read my manuscript. My most
grateful appreciation goes to my editor, Linda Zuckerman, who knew long
before I did that there was more than one book to be written about patchwork patterns.
I couldn't have done this book without any of you.

Requests for permission to make copies of any part of the work should be mailed to:
Permissions Department, Harcourt Brace & Company,
6277 Sea Harbor Drive, Orlando, Florida 32887-6777.

Browndeer Press is a registered trademark of Harcourt Brace & Company.

Library of Congress Cataloging-in-Publication Data
Paul, Ann Whitford.
The seasons sewn: a year in patchwork/by Ann Whitford Paul;
illustrated by Michael McCurdy.—1st ed.
p.   cm.
"Browndeer Press."
ISBN 0-15-276918-8
1. Patchwork—United States—Patterns—Juvenile literature. 2. Quilting—United States—
Patterns—Juvenile literature. 3. Frontier and pioneer life—United States—Juvenile literature.
[1. Patchwork. 2. Quilts. 3. Frontier and pioneer life.]
I. McCurdy, Michael. II. Title.
TT835.P387   1996
746.46'0973—dc20   94-35358

B D F G E C
Printed in Singapore

Introduction

If you were a young child in this country during the first one hundred years after the signing of the Declaration of Independence, you very likely lived with your parents and several brothers and sisters in a small home of maybe just one room. The walls could have been rough logs; the floor, packed-down dirt. Looking out of any window, you probably couldn't see another house.

Because you lived so far away from people and the nearest town, your family had to make, raise, grow, or hunt much of what it needed to survive. Your life was linked to the seasons, and when they changed, so did many of your activities.

Spring with its melting snow and softening earth was the season of planting and marked the beginning of a new farming year. Your father and brothers hurried to finish clearing the land of trees, shrubs, and rocks. Then they plowed the earth and, walking up and down each long row, dropped seeds and covered them with dirt. Several times a day you helped patrol the freshly planted fields, chasing away hungry birds.

Your mother continued her year-round work of preparing all the family's meals. While she kneaded bread dough, you stirred a stew bubbling in its pot in the large hearth. Your mother took advantage of the warm spring days to thoroughly clean your home—airing out quilts and carpets and sweeping under furniture. Eagerly she looked forward to the time when the "road," often only a small dirt footpath, would be dry enough for her to travel several hours to visit friends she hadn't seen for a long time.

Then came summer, the season when those seeds your father and brothers had planted began to grow. So did the weeds. After your father and brothers finished pulling out the uninvited plants, they used the extra hours of sunshine to add a second room to the house or to patch the barn roof.

The longer days gave your mother time to catch up on her never-ending job of making and mending the family's clothing. Summer made her washing day easier, too, because after you helped her scrub the clothes clean, she could hang them up on a line or spread them over bushes to dry in the hot sun.

Perhaps during the summer your entire family got into your horse-drawn wagon and visited your grandparents in the city a hundred miles away. It took you at least five days to get there. One night your father probably stopped by the side of the road and everyone slept under the stars, but on another night, a kind family invited you in to share their supper and made room for you to sleep on their floor.

The city where your grandparents lived was not large. You could probably walk or ride a horse across it in one day. Your grandfather might have owned a small general store, but still he and your grandmother kept a garden for growing foods like pumpkins, beans, and squash, and herbs like sage and thyme. In his general store, he sold all kinds of things— ribbons and coffee beans and looking glasses. He rarely took money from his customers for their purchases; instead, they "paid" him in kind with a handmade broom or a basket of eggs or by doing some service he needed.

When it was time to leave, you hated to say good-bye because you knew it might be years before you would make the long trip to see your grandparents again.

Once you returned home, you were busy harvesting crops. Often there was so much work your family invited friends and neighbors from miles around to help pick your corn or apples. Grateful for the chance to visit, everyone usually stayed for a big meal and played music and danced late into the night.

Your father and brothers hunted, and your mother dried or smoked the meats they brought home. She preserved fruits and vegetables so the family would have plenty to eat all winter. She also made candles to brighten your house in the long evenings to come.

Then the weather turned cold and snow began to fall. With less demand for your help at home, you and your brothers and sisters bundled up and walked several miles to the nearest school. You probably sat in one room, with students of all ages learning together. At the end of the day, maybe your teacher came home with you, because a part of her wages was paid in room and board.

Your mother and father spent much of the winter inside, pulling chairs close to the warmth and light of the hearth. Possibly your father repaired the handle on his cross saw or carved decorative legs for a new chair. Your mother used the wool she'd spun into yarn at her spinning wheel and knitted sweaters and mittens. She darned socks and mended dresses. Sometimes when school was out, your sisters, too, sat at her side and practiced making tiny, even stitches to prepare for the time when they would be mothers sewing clothes for their families.

All year, no matter what the season, your days began when the sun first shone and ended soon after the sun went down. You fell asleep exhausted from your hard labors and with more of the same to look forward to the next day. Only Sunday was different. Then you and your family would go to church.

When you had some time to relax away from your chores, possibly you played with a seven-piece puzzle, trying to see how many different shapes you could make with the pieces. Maybe your sister sewed a doll and your brother whittled a duck. Your father might have read or told you stories while your mother did her fine sewing—embroidery, crewel, and patchwork.

Patchwork is the stitching together of small pieces of fabric into squares called blocks. Many of the different names given to patterns reflect the way families' lives across the country were connected to nature and the seasons.

If you had lived a long time ago, your sisters might have helped your mother make fabric—washing, carding, spinning, dyeing, and weaving threads into a cloth—or your mother may have bought factory-made cloth. This was expensive, and although some women could afford to buy new material for each new quilt, your mother often used pieces left over from her other sewing projects.

The blocks of patchwork were sewn together into a large square and, with a backing material and a sheet of cotton or wool called batting, made into a warm quilt. The beautiful designs of her patchwork quilts added color and decoration to your plain home. Maybe you sewed patchwork, too. Some children made their first quilts when they were only five years old!

What can the patchwork patterns and their names tell us about the seasons and early life in this country?

Spring

Album

MANY WEDDINGS took place before the hard work of planting began. When a young woman was about to marry and move to a new home, maybe far away, her friends often sewed her a present of an album quilt. Each one stitched a block, sometimes using leftover fabric from a favorite dress, and signed her name in the center with thread or indelible ink. After the blocks were joined into one big square, everyone sat around a large quilting frame and stitched it into a quilt. Then no matter how many miles or years separated the friends, the bride could look at her quilt, run her hand over the familiar fabrics and names, and remember those she had left behind.

Crossed Canoes

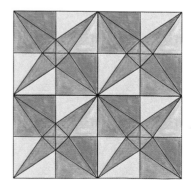

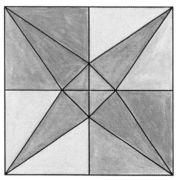

NATIVE AMERICANS in the north, central, and eastern regions of our country traveled the newly thawed lakes and rivers in small, light canoes. Those living in the Northwest needed bigger, heavier ones for fishing in the rough Pacific Ocean, so they made theirs by hollowing out tree trunks, sometimes fifty feet long. When the explorer Captain James Cook sailed along the northwest coast in 1778, he was greeted by many native men paddling together in these giant canoes. They crossed back and forth in front of his ship, just as the canoes cross on this patchwork. The native men chanted words no one on board could understand. Soon, though, using body and sign language, they made their wishes known and began to trade sea otter skins, handmade spears, and fishhooks for buttons, knives, and looking glasses from the explorers.

Bear's Paw

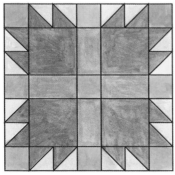

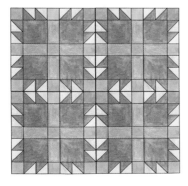

TRAMPING ALONE through the woods to check his traps for beavers, a trapper might have seen large paw tracks in the mud. He would have looked around nervously, knowing he had to be extra careful because a bear had awakened from its hibernation and was probably starving. Sometimes the bear surprised him by lumbering out from behind a clump of trees. It stood up on its hind legs. Its sharp teeth glistened and its roar thundered. It raised its clawed paws, ready to strike. If he could, the trapper shot and killed the bear with his rifle. Then for many nights to come he would enjoy tasty bear meat suppers. This design looks like the paw print the trapper saw in the mud.

Dolley Madison Star

THE **WIFE** of James Madison, president of the United States from 1809–1817, invited the children of Washington, D.C., to the country's first Easter egg roll. Each child brought baskets of brightly colored, hard-boiled eggs to the Capitol grounds on the Monday after Easter. Some went to the top of the gently terraced land and began rolling their eggs to the others waiting at the bottom. Down the grassy slopes, the eggs slid and bounced and bumped. The girls and boys below grabbed any that didn't crack and ran up to roll them again. When their eggs were all broken, many children started rolling and somersaulting down the hill themselves. Maybe a young girl worked this pattern to thank the First Lady for the wonderful time she had one Easter Monday.

Tea Leaf

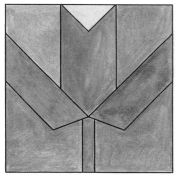

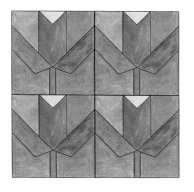

WHEN SPRING showers were over and the roads no longer muddy, many women put on their best dresses and walked—or rode their horses or buggies—to have tea at the home of a friend. In the South and Northeast, where the house might be grand, the woman was invited into the parlor, a room reserved for guests. Chairs and tables, usually lined against the wall, were moved into the center of the room. Then the women sat and drank their steaming hot tea. They ate sweet cakes and talked about what had happened in their lives since they had last been together. Because they enjoyed this special time so much and knew that months might pass before they saw one another again, their visit could last for hours. Perhaps one woman returned home after having tea with a friend and started sewing this patchwork, recalling their pleasant conversation with each small stitch.

The Trail of the Covered Wagon

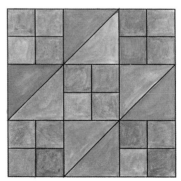

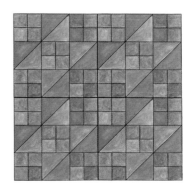

PIONEERS HEADING toward the West Coast waited until the prairie grasses had grown tall enough to feed their livestock. Then they loaded their belongings into a covered wagon. They stowed cooking and eating utensils and enough food for a five-month journey—sacks of flour, tins of coffee, hams, and dried fruits. They packed a tent, warm quilts, one change of clothing, and tools for repairing the wagon and building a new home. There were always some things not useful but too cherished to leave—Grandmother's pewter pitcher, the family Bible, a comfortable rocking chair. The wagon, frequently pulled by a team of oxen, was so full, most of the family had to walk. And it was so heavy, its wheels cut ruts in the ground. The wagons that followed cut the ruts deeper. Possibly a woman looking at the trail her wagon left behind imagined this pattern.

Summer

Baseball

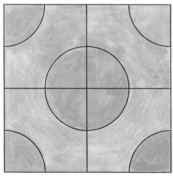

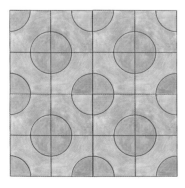

IN THE MID-1800s, young men got together in clubs to play an early form of baseball. Spectators sat on horses or in carriages at the edge of the field. A player on one team pitched the ball to a player on the other who tried to hit it with his wooden bat. If the players in the field caught the ball in the air, or after only one bounce, the batter was out. But they played bare-handed, and sometimes the force of the ball stung their palms or broke a bone in their fingers. Then the fielder dropped the ball and the batter was safe. Maybe a young woman on the sidelines saw her brother make a difficult game-winning catch and honored him by working this design.

Job's Troubles

AFTER EVERYONE'S chores were done, many children took advantage of the longer days to practice their reading. The Bible was often the only book a family owned, and one of the stories they read out loud was about Job, whose faith in God was tested by a series of terrible troubles. Job's livestock were stolen. His children died. And his body was covered with painful ulcers. In spite of his great suffering, Job still worshiped God, and eventually his steadfastness was rewarded. A father listening to his children read in their strong, clear voices might have looked around at his well-built cabin and his wife busily sewing her patchwork; whatever problems he had must have seemed small compared to Job's. Perhaps from that day forth, whenever he looked at his wife's patchwork, he felt grateful for his family's many blessings.

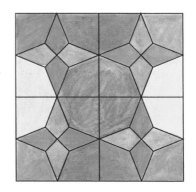

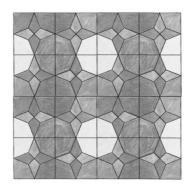

Blazing Star

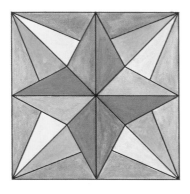

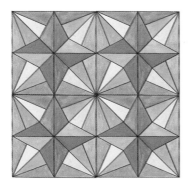

BELLS RANG and cannons fired in cities and small towns every Fourth of July morning to announce our nation's birthday celebration. Families traveled for miles and gathered in the town square, or at the courthouse steps, and listened to men read the Declaration of Independence and deliver patriotic speeches. Afterward, bands, soldiers, and decorated buggies paraded down the street. Then there were big picnics and wagon races and maybe a ball game and a square dance, too. When the sun went down and the night turned black, fireworks often lit up the sky. The bursts of bright, blazing stars looked like the stars of this pattern.

Fish Block

WHILE SOME boys fished with poles or nets, others fished with guns. A boy would sit on the riverbank and wait to see the ripples that meant a school of fish was swimming his way. Quickly, he put his gun on the water's surface and fired. The bullet didn't need to hit or kill a fish because the shock of the explosion stunned all those within a wide area, and they floated belly-up to the top. The boy gathered as many fish as he could and then attached them to a long rope to carry home. Perhaps a mother worked this design to celebrate all the wonderful food her son caught for the family.

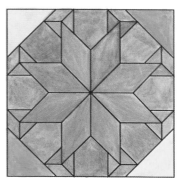

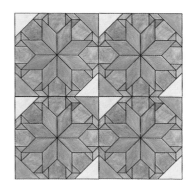

Corn and Beans

A PIONEER FAMILY passing through a place where a group of Native American people lived often saw fields of corn growing nearby. They might also have seen vines of beans climbing up the tall, straight cornstalks. Native Americans frequently planted corn and beans together. They cooked them together, too. Once in a while, a friendly chief invited the pioneers to stop for the night and eat some of the corn-and-bean stew, called succotash. It tasted so good that when the family finally reached their destination, the daughter could have sewn this pattern to remind her of the delicious new food she'd tasted.

Mariner's Compass

L ARGE SHIPS sailed the oceans in search of whales. Whale blubber was boiled down into oil for people to burn in lamps. Whalebones were used for stays in ladies' corsets and ribs in their umbrellas. Several years often passed before the men on board, called mariners, had killed enough of the huge mammals and were ready to start home. But which way was home? Water stretched on and on to the horizon in every direction. Although they could figure out which way to go by studying the sun or stars, sometimes the thick clouds of a late August storm blocked them all out. Then the mariner used a compass with thirty-two directional points, the same number of points as in this patchwork. A needle in the center, attracted by the magnetic pull of the North Pole, always pointed north, making it easy to know where to steer the ship.

Fall

Broken Dishes

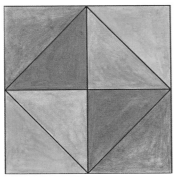

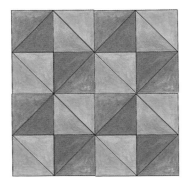

PIONEERS HEADING toward the West Coast planned to start crossing the Sierra Nevada by early September. The mountains were steep and treacherous, and the oxen pulling the wagons often stumbled. The wheels snapped in two. Many times the wagon toppled over, tumbling out all the family's possessions. Tools bounced out of sight; clothes caught on bushes; dried fruits were caked with mud; and flour blew away with the wind. A woman might have picked up a shattered piece of china she'd carefully brought all the way from the East. Sadly, she turned it over and over in her hand. Maybe she whispered, "Something good must come of this," and later stitched this design.

Rising Star

AFRICAN AMERICANS held in slavery often chose the last warm time of the year to try to escape to the North, where they could be free. They waited until the stars seemed to rise in the sky, and they always stayed away from the main roads. Using the bright North Star as their guide, they tramped through thick woods, grassy meadows, and soggy swamps. Sometimes they waded in streams and swam across rivers. When morning came, they hid in caves, under bridges, or beneath a haystack so they wouldn't be caught and returned to their owners. It's possible a courageous African American woman sewed this patchwork, remembering the North Star and her escape to freedom.

Cake Stand

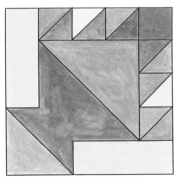

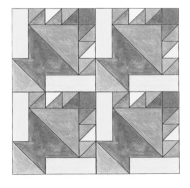

FRIENDS AND neighbors frequently got together to help one another harvest their ripe apples. All the women brought foods they had prepared earlier at home—boiled hams, roasted chickens, breads, cooked turnips, potatoes, and corn puddings. They always brought lots of desserts—pies and cookies, pound cakes, spice cakes, and chocolate cakes, too. Whole families came and everyone worked, either picking the apples or peeling them for later drying. By the time they finished, the men, women, boys, and girls were all hungry and hurried to serve themselves from the tables laden with platters, bowls, baskets of food, and cake stands that looked like this pattern.

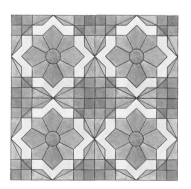

T W O   M E N running for the U.S. Senate from Illinois met several times during the fall of 1858 to debate. Whole communities came to hear them, even though only white men were allowed to vote. Stephen A. Douglas, up for reelection, was a short man and a powerful speaker. People called him Little Giant. His opponent, Abraham Lincoln, stood a full head taller. For three hours from a wooden platform decorated with flags and brightly colored banners, Douglas and Lincoln shouted to make themselves heard by the audience of a few thousand people. Although women could not vote, they still had strong opinions about the election. Working this patchwork, a woman could let others know which candidate was her favorite.

Turkey Tracks

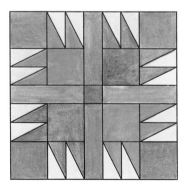

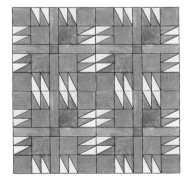

EACH FALL New England farmers hired men called drovers to take their turkeys to the faraway city markets. Sometimes the drovers had only a hundred turkeys, sometimes several hundred. They herded the large, noisy birds day after day, up and down mountains, across meadows, and through woods. When the turkeys tried to stop, the drover prodded them with a pole, or whistled, or clapped, or rang a loud bell, and they started moving again. But when night came, everyone rested. Some turkeys slept on the branches of a tree or on the roof of a nearby barn or house. Others stayed on the ground. Possibly a woman, finding her house surrounded by dozing turkeys, noticed their tracks and stitched this design.

Jack-in-the-Pulpit

MANY WOMEN, living miles away from the nearest doctor, gathered different wild plants and mixed their roots and leaves into medicines for their families. They used recipes passed down from their mothers or taught to them by Native American people. When an early snow and wind storm made a mother's children shiver with cold and shake from coughing, she took out of a small tin a pinch of dried and powdered root from the jack-in-the-pulpit plant. She mixed it with liquid and made each child swallow the bitter cough medicine. Perhaps someone, grateful to the jack-in-the-pulpit plant for curing her children, sewed this patchwork.

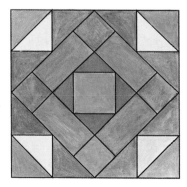

Winter

Mixed T

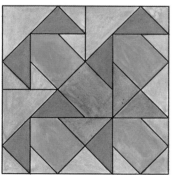

SCHOOLS OPENED in the winter months when children were not needed at home to help with the chores of harvesting and planting. But in the South before the Civil War, African American boys and girls held in slavery were never allowed to attend school. If their master discovered someone teaching them, he would severely punish both the student and the teacher. Yet some brave children wanted to learn. When they had to accompany their master's children and carry their books to the schoolhouse, they could spend the long hours until school was over sitting under an open window, listening to everything being taught inside. They could also stand on their tiptoes and watch the teacher write on the blackboard. Maybe one African American child practiced writing the letter *T* with a stick in the dirt and then later stitched scraps of cloth together into this pattern.

Falling Timbers

W HEN A PIONEER family chose a site in the woods for their new home, it was necessary to clear away the towering trees. The father picked up his ax and swung at one of the trunks. He swung again and again and again. Finally he heard a loud crack, and the tree swayed and thundered to the ground. The man had to chop down many trees to build a cabin. Then he had to clear away more trees to make a field for planting crops. He cut down more to use to build his barn and his fences. And every day his wife needed wood for her cooking fire. The crash of falling timbers could be heard all year round. It's possible a woman thought of this design as she watched her husband go out in the freezing cold to chop down yet another tree.

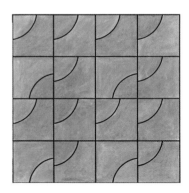

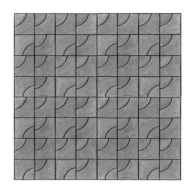

Reel

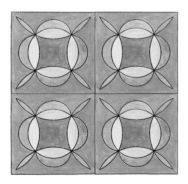

O N C O L D D A Y S women often moved their spinning wheels in front of the warm hearth and spun different fibers like flax and wool into thread. The wheel, turned either by hand or a foot pedal, hummed as it went around and around. Soon a woman would have a bobbin full of thread or yarn and was ready to wind it into big loops, called skeins, which she would later dye different colors. Often she asked her children to hold out their arms so she could loop the yarn around them. But sometimes her husband would make her a reel to help with the winding. A young girl watching her mother learn to use her new reel could have imagined this pattern.

Beautiful Star

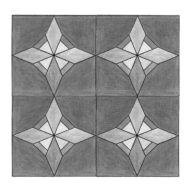

T H E C U S T O M of decorating a tree at Christmas was brought over to this country by settlers from Germany, but it didn't gain popularity right away. The few families that did have a tree usually chopped down a small one in a nearby woods and dragged it home to stand in a container on top of a table. The parents closed the door so the children couldn't see them decorate it with animal-shaped cookies; strands of popcorn and cranberries; small, unwrapped presents like a homemade doll or a pair of mittens; and one or more stars made of tin. They attached candles to the branches, lit them, and then opened the door for the children to run in. The beautiful way a tin star reflected a candle's flame might have inspired a young girl to sew this patchwork.

Fox and Geese

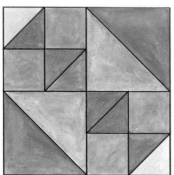

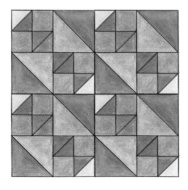

WHEN SNOW covered the ground with a thick, white blanket, some boys and girls stayed inside and played a board game called fox and geese. Other children dressed up in their warmest clothes and went outside to play a different game *also* known as fox and geese. They tramped down the snow into a large circle path with spokes that met in the center. Then one child was chosen to be the fox; everyone else was a goose. The first goose tagged by the fox became the new fox, so everyone ran as fast as possible to stay away from him. No players, fox or geese, could run outside of a path. If a goose did, she was automatically the new fox. If the fox ran outside the path, he was doubly punished by having to catch two geese before he could stop being "it." Perhaps someone remembering the good time she'd had playing fox and geese worked this pattern.

Pine Tree

MANY FATHERS built their own one-room houses and, using the wood from the pine tree, made the furniture that went inside it. They built a table and benches and a chest to store quilts in. They also built a bed. In most houses, two, three, four, or more children slept together, snuggled warm and close. Maybe one cold night a young girl awakened with an elbow in her chest or a knee in her stomach. But since the only heat came from small embers in the fireplace far across the room, she didn't complain. She was grateful for the coziness of her pine wood bed. Maybe she fell back to sleep and dreamed of the coming spring. Or maybe she dreamed of this design.

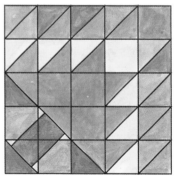

Conclusion

T<small>HE OLD</small> patchwork patterns tell of life and the seasons during the time they were created. Today many women and girls, maybe even a few men and boys, sew patchwork. Some use the same patterns stitched long ago. Others make up their own patterns. You can look at new patchworks and guess what they will tell future generations about our life and the way we lived our seasons.

  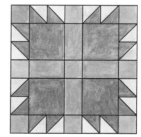

AUTHOR'S NOTE

WHEN A woman saw a new patchwork pattern she wanted to try, it was frequently pieced in a quilt lying on a friend's bed. Without pattern books and with little paper to sketch on, she would try to memorize the design. Memories weren't always accurate. This may explain why there are often several variations of the same patchwork. Also, the same patterns were sometimes given different names depending on the region of the country where they were stitched. In this book, I have tried to use the design that over the years has been most associated with a particular patchwork name.

Over 160 books and periodicals were used in researching the material for *The Seasons Sewn*. The following bibliography includes books you might enjoy for further reading about patchwork and long ago life.

SELECTED BIBLIOGRAPHY

Drepperd, Carl W. *Pioneer America: Its First Three Centuries.* Garden City, NY: Doubleday & Company, Inc., 1949.

Eaton, Herbert. *The Overland Trail to California in 1852.* New York: G. P. Putnam's Sons, 1974.

Feldstein, Stanley. *Once a Slave: The Slaves' View of Slavery.* New York: William Morrow and Company, Inc., 1971.

Garrett, Elisabeth Donaghy. *At Home: The American Family 1750–1870.* New York: Harry N. Abrams Inc., Publisher, 1990.

Hall, Carrie A., and Rose G. Kretsinger. *The Romance of the Patchwork Quilt in America.* New York: Bonanza Books, 1935.

Kiracofe, Roderick. Text with Mary Elizabeth Johnson. *The American Quilt: A History of Cloth and Comfort 1740–1950.* New York: Clarkson Potter Publishers, 1993.

Larkin, Jack. *The Reshaping of Everyday Life: 1790–1840.* New York: Harper & Row, Publishers, 1988.

Lipsett, Linda Otto. *Remember Me: Women & Their Friendship Quilts.* San Francisco: The Quilt Digest Press, 1985.

Schlissel, Lillian. *Women's Diaries of the Westward Journey.* New York: Schocken Books, 1982.

Stratton, Joanna L. *Pioneer Women: Voices from the Kansas Frontier.* New York: Simon & Schuster, 1981.

The illustrations in this book were done in colored scratchboard on Rising Photolene paper.
The display type was set in Columbus Semi Bold by Harcourt Brace & Company
Photocomposition Center, San Diego, California.
The text type was set in Granjon by Thompson Type, San Diego, California.
Color separations by Bright Arts, Ltd., Singapore
Printed and bound by Tien Wah Press, Singapore
Production supervision by Warren Wallerstein and Pascha Gerlinger
Designed by Lori J. McThomas